CW01090974

DEPRESS__

A SELF-HELP BOOK THAT DEALS WITH
DEPRESSION, BIPOLAR AND ANXIETY
DISORDERS, TREATMENTS, MEDICATIONS
AND NATURAL REMEDIES.

A.L.HARLOW

DISCLAIMER AND TERMS OF USE AGREEMENT:

This information presented in this book has not been prepared by a medical practitioner and is to be used for education and information. Never ignore the advice of a medical professional or put off seeking advice.

The authors offer no warranties regarding the accuracy or completeness of this book.

If you wish to use any ideas contained in this book you are assuming responsibility for your actions.

Neither the author nor the publisher will be held liable for any direct, indirect, punitive or consequential damages arising from the use of any the material, contained in this book. This book is provided without warranties.

This work is © Copyrighted by A.L.HARLOW. No part of this work may be copied, or changed in any format, or used in any way other than what is outlined in this book. Any violations would be prosecuted severely.

Table of Contents

Introduction

Has depression taken away the enthusiasm and zest you once had? Have you forgotten the feeling of true happiness?

If you can answer yes to those two questions then you should read this book. If you have a loved one or friend who you think would answer yes to those two questions then you should read this book.

Depression destroys you slowly, don't let it steal your life away.

This disease affects people from all walks of life. Look at this list of famous people who suffered with depression yet still did great things with their lives.

Winston Churchill - Prime Minister of Great Britain.

Patty Duke - Bipolar.

Linda Hamilton –Bipolar

Abraham Lincoln

Isaac Newton - had several "nervous breakdowns" and great fits of rage.

Jimmy Piersall – Bipolar

Brooke Shields - postpartum depression

Vincent Van Gogh - unstable moods accompanied by manic episodes. He committed suicide aged 37.

Ludwig Von Beethoven – Bipolar disorder.

Jane Pauley – Bipolar.

Terry Bradshaw.

HISTORICAL UNDERSTANDINGS OF DEPRESSION

There has never been a time in history when depression was not a health problem for people.

Many documents have been written by healers, writers and philosophers throughout history that point to existence of depression.

Melancholia was the initial term used to describe depression and the earliest reports come from ancient Mesopotamian texts. Back then, melancholia was blamed on demonic possession. Thus, the first interpretation of depression was that it was a spiritual illness not a physical one.

Among the ancient Greeks and Romans thinking was divided as to the causes of melancholia. At that time, literature was packed with writings about melancholia being caused by spirits or demons. Other early civilizations including Babylon, China and Egypt also considered melancholia to be a form of demonic possession. The treatment prescribed was beatings, restraint, and starvation with the intent of driving the demons out of the body of the possessed person. Differing in opinion were the early Roman and Greek doctors who believed it was both biological and psychological. The Roman and Greek doctors prescribed massage, music, baths and special diets along with a concoction made from the extract of poppies and donkey's to alleviate the melancholic symptoms.

A Greek physician named Hippocrates thought that mental illness and personality traits were caused by an imbalance of bodily fluids which he called humors. Four of these humors were documented; black bile, phlegm, yellow bile and blood. Hippocrates further classified mental illness into categories. These categories included melancholia, mania and brain fever. Hippocrates believed melancholia was the result of too much black bile in the spleen and he used bloodletting, exercising, bathing, and dieting to treat the symptoms. In contrast the famous Roman philosopher Cicero professed that melancholia was the result of fear, rage and grief. Cicero's was a mental rather than physical explanation.

Hippocrates influence faded in the final years before Christ and the prevailing belief among cultured Romans was that depression and other forms of mental illnesses were caused by the anger of gods and demons. Cornelius Celsus for instance, believed that shackles, beating and starvation were appropriate treatments. The Persian physician Rhazes, who was the head doctor at Baghdad hospital, in contrast to the Roman view, saw the brain as the center of both mental illness and depression. His treatments involved behavior therapy, rewards for good behavior and hydrotherapy.

During the 14th century when the renaissance began in Italy considerations of mental illness was regarded as both progressive and regressive. Witch-hunts and executions of mentally ill persons were common and conversely some doctors reverted to the Hippocratic views, positively stating that the causes of mental illnesses were natural and that the witches themselves were mentally ill people in need medical treatment.

Anatomy of Melancholy was published by Robert Burton In 1621. In this work, Burton described both psychological and social causes such as fear, poverty and solitude as sources of depression. In his work, the treatment recommended was exercise, diet, travel, distraction, blood-letting, purgatives to remove toxins in the body, bloodletting, music, herbal remedies and marriage.

At the onset of the Age of Enlightenment, depression was thought to be an inherited and resolute weakness of disposition, this in turn led to the belief that people affected with depression should be spurned or locked away. The result of this belief was that most people suffering from mental illnesses became poor and homeless with some being sent to institutions.

Thankfully we have made a lot of progress in treating depression.

SIGNS AND SYMPTOMS

As in the past, depression, is considered to be more a not so much a variety of moods and conditions rather than a particular illness. None of us will ever go through life without feeling sad at some time by the death of a loved one, the break-up of a relationship, or some other disappointment. Depression due to events such as these is perfectly normal, and unless it is long-standing would not require medical intervention.

Nowadays we see long-term depression, in all its forms, as being a condition of the brain and as such, being treatable, through the correction of chemical imbalances in the brain.

While we see depression as a mental ailment, that is not 100% true. It has been said that the reverse of depression is not so much happiness as it is liveliness. Acute depression often causes lethargy and world-weariness; some people even end up being bed-ridden.

THE NATIONAL INSTITUTE OF MENTAL HEALTH LISTS THE FOLLOWING SYMPTOMS OF DEPRESSION:

Difficulty concentrating
Difficulty remembering details

Difficulty making decisions
Feeling fatigued and lacking energy
Feeling guilty, worthless and helpless
Feeling hopeless or pessimistic
Insomnia
Early-morning wakefulness
Excessive sleeping
Irritability
Restlessness
Lost interest in activities
Lost interest in hobbies
Lost interest in sex
Overeating
Loss of appetite
Persistent sadness
Persistent anxiety
Persistent feelings of emptiness
Thoughts of suicide
Attempted suicide

THE IMPORTANCE OF FAMILY AND FRIEND'S SUPPORT

The importance of support and understanding of family and friends cannot be understated.

It is difficult for people suffering from depression to live normally. Every aspect of their life can and will be affected. They may be too tired to give at home or even at work. They can and often will be disinterested in a healthy diet, sex, responsible parenting or exercising. Worse, depression can and does reduce or even obliterate their sense of happiness and joy.

People suffering with depression often feel overcome and unable to cope with all of their symptoms. Unsurprisingly, they also feel a lot of guilt also. They are aware that their lack of interest is a burden on everyone else. It's not uncommon for them to feel guilty about letting other people down but they are unable to change. I remember well the attitude of my wife and children who thought I was an asshole who was often angry and always distant. More than once friends of my wife would ask why she stayed with me, more than once the neighbor's kids asked why I was always angry, I never understood why they felt that way and was powerless to change it. It was only after I was finally given the right medicine that I was able to look back at my life and see the problems and accept them as mine.

Both family members and Friends will find themselves dealing with a gamut emotions living with someone who is depressed.

Frustration – I can understand why people feel irritated when a person isn't doing their share, doesn't fulfill obligations, or can't even finish little simple things.

Anger – It's common that the person may function well at work, but not function well and experience more acute symptom, and take them out on people around them when they are at home. For families living with someone suffering from depression this is a common source of anger and conflict.

Confusion – is not like a broken leg, it's not often easy to comprehend the limits of people suffering depression. A couple of oft asked questions are:

Why don't they help out around the house? Why don't they attend a school function?

It can also be difficult to be aware of when it's applicable to discuss your personal needs when the depressed person seems so introverted.

Withdrawals – similar to the way a depressed person retreats from activities and seems introverted, families can and do pull away also. They look for new ways of operating without the person.

Anxiety -- It's normal to be anxious about when or if the depressed person ever be "normal" again.

Guilt – sometimes family members feel some responsibility for being the cause of the problem and sometimes they feel guilty about the frustration they are undergoing.

WHAT CAN WE DO?

Acknowledge that depression is not just a "bad mood". Depression is a real illness. It is a challenging and exasperating condition that affects the individual and everyone who cares about the person. It takes a substantial amount of work on not just the patient but the entire family to overcome and recover from, the influence of depression.

Acknowledge a starting point. Depression can exacerbate existing negative family dynamics. Family underlying forces can make it more difficult for the patient and the family to make the requisite changes to win the battle with depression. On the other hand, a full recovery will not inevitably resolve every family problem.

Promote a team attitude. A person suffering from depression often feels completely alone. In truth, the entire family often feels isolated. To confirm to the depressed person that you intend to work together by adopting a partnership to overcome the hurdles that lie ahead.

Don't try to assign blame to anyone. It's normal to want to attach blame to someone when things go awry or trials seem unbeatable. But recovery can only begin when the blaming stops. No one person is responsible for the manifestation of depression.

Know that the symptoms the depressed person who is suffering along with side effects from medication, may suppress his/her capabilities. Simultaneously know that you cannot do everything. Rank daily chores, activities and responsibilities, realizing full well that not everything may get done. It is also helpful to look for smaller more manageable ways to make improvements, such as making mealtimes more enjoyable.

While considering your personal necessities, help the depressed person address their needs too. It may be beneficial to read some articles for ideas on ways to build patience, improve communication and deal etc. A counselor is often helpful in helping everyone to develop better communications skills.

Emotions are a regular component of daily life in every family. However, you must not emotions become too intense or interfere too often. For instance, when one family member is nagging or complaining, another family member may become angry and withdrawn. Although these are understandable reactions, they do not help. Instead of corking feelings until the pressure is too great and they eventually explode, seek ways to express your emotions without criticism or hostility. Constructive criticism is a contradiction in terms.

Communicate with the depressed person about things you could do together that you would enjoy as a couple or a family. Always bear in mind that it is the thought behind the gesture that is key. A simple walk or watching a movie together can deliver a needed breather and provide a diversion for all.

Depressed, people often have no interest in exercise. But even modest activity such as a brief walk, can produce positive benefits immediately. Inspire the depressed person to do some exercise by proposing to join them, and making a promise to do more exercise together.

Support groups exist for family members, friends and care providers of people suffering with depression. Ask about one near you as a way to join with others in the same boat as you. You could also explore the possibilities of help and support that may be obtainable through social services or churches. These may include child care, meal services and counseling, to assist you in better managing the needs of your domiciliary.

LOOKING OUT FOR YOURSELF

You must take care of yourself before you can consider caring for someone else.

In this section, I have outlined strategies that recognize the importance of the caregiver getting self-care as well as the person who is depressed. It is important as a caregiver to identify and realize both the depressed person's health and your health are linked. The depressed person's anguish can become your anguish. Recent research studies have shown that up to 40% of people living with someone suffering depression may themselves be distressed enough to require psychological intervention.

Treatments for Depression Without Side Effects

The rates of depression worldwide have increased at an alarming rate since the end of World War II.

Severe depression destroys both lives and families. Many people try and have tried several forms of treatment before realizing any improvement. Many others are not so blessed and pay the definitive price. Drugs and medication have received a lot of criticism in recent years. This criticism is primarily over the quantity of medication being taken. There are natural treatments for depression and they should be tried first if at all possible.

Sleeping soundly through the night is crucial. There is a close link between sleep and mood. Tired people react to things differently than they do when they have had plenty of rest.

Stimulants and caffeine are better avoided. They do provide short term energy boosts but are known to deplete the levels of serotonin in the brain. It is claimed that low serotonin levels are the principal cause of depression.

I suggest you take one multivitamin every day. If your life style dictates that you skip meals this is very important. A deficiency of some vitamins has been connected to depression.

Some sufferers get in touch with their spiritual side, you may want to try getting in touch with your spiritual side too. This can be done in a couple of ways; attending church is a good opportunity, as is prayer and meditation. One does not need to be religious to be spiritual. My preference is meditation but there are many paths, fishing and hiking are just two.

So, consider getting more exercise. Not decathlon, start small and build up as you improve your fitness. Endorphins are released during while you are exercising and endorphins make you feel more enabled. There are added health benefits from exercise so that is a bonus.

Treating depression with the natural approach isn't always the most effective way but if your symptoms are not too severe and you are not suicidal or debilitated, then at least give it a try.

There are a number of natural pills and potions you can try before resorting to prescribed drugs. St. John's Wort has been tried by many and it has been known to improve the mood of some people suffering from depression.

People suffering from depression should avoid drinking too much alcohol. Many depressed people drink to drown their misery but it does not work. Alcohol as a depressant slows down your body. Alcohol can react with the chemistry of your body and worsens your condition. Additionally, alcohol is also a poison that no healthy body needs.

Vitamin and mineral deficiencies are linked to depression so strive to eat a balanced diet. You will never have a balanced diet eating at restaurants such as McDonald's. Make time to eat no matter what your lifestyle is.

Cognitive behavior therapy will aid you in refocusing your thinking thereby generating more positive feelings. What you think affects your mood. The more negative thoughts you have the worse your depression will become.

Stress management training could help you if you lead a taxing lifestyle. Stress can be the precursor of many illnesses other than depression. Having the knowledge and skill to cope with stressful situations will help your depression.

Volunteering and helping others less fortunate can be quite gratifying and can cancel out many negative thoughts you have about yourself.

If you find the natural approach does not work don't feel bad. If taking medications is the answer, that's fine.

If you have a loved one struggling with depression, it is normal to want to assist them. You can be incredibly supportive for someone suffering from depression. However, you must have the knowledge and skill to make a difference. Without the knowledge and skill you can do more harm than good.

To begin you should learn everything you can about treatment for depression. By gaining some knowledge, you can help a depressed person make right decisions when they are not incapable. Learning as much as you can about the effects of depression helps you to get through the bad days.

You must always be aware that caring for someone who is depressed person will deplete you both emotionally and physically. You MUST set aside some time for you. You will be of no help to your loved one if you are feeling stressed and tired. The truth is you could actually exacerbate their problem. Talk to someone who is sympathetic to your situation about what you about what you are going through or even possibly even join a support group. Take some time to entertain yourself and have some fun, don't let the depression of your loved one control your life.

A depressed person needs a lot of love and support. Don't smother them but be there when they need you most. Knowing they have your support and love will help them through some of the worst times.

Never deny your own emotional state at the times you're feeling most angry and frustrated. A support network is crucial to help you get these feelings off your chest. Bottling up your own feelings can lead to you too becoming depressed.

TALKING THERAPIES

Dealing with a depressed person, to say the least, is challenging and draining. In addition to the person who is depressed it will put stress on those close to him or her. It may be necessary to try many therapies before any improvement is evident. One possible therapy is "Talk Therapy".

Talking therapies can be very beneficial when treating depression. It involves various forms of psychological counseling. Talking therapies encourage depressed people to vent their feelings. Talking therapies also allow for the patient and councilor to work as a team to try to discover the basic cause of the depression.

Talking therapies do differ but in general involve the same fundamental foundations. First the therapist listens to the depressed person's problems. In time the depressed person will develop a relationship with their therapist and begin to feel the therapist understands them. What follows is emotional release; emotional release can be helpful but must not be done too often. The release of emotions too often can lead to further depression. Then come advice and guidance. Finally, there is the information you gave. Initially information is given in small doses but as the therapy progresses this can be increased. People who are depressed often have poor concentration and memory information is doled out very carefully.

These talking therapies can be very helpful when treating depression but they are not quick fixes. It may need many sessions involving both the patient and family. Talking therapies can be very beneficial in mild to moderate depression but severe cases of depression will almost certainly require medication also.

ECT Therapies

We know more about depression today than ever before and more treatment methods are available. Additionally, medications to help people function as normally as possible are available.

Depression is a debilitating illness and unlike most physical illnesses, it can take a long time before any improvement is noticeable. Though there are many therapies available there are still a few people that seem to be outside the reach of most conventional therapies. When nothing else seems to help ECT therapy is an option.

The decision to give ECT therapy isn't taken lightly. It is normally as a last resort if all other therapies have failed. It is only administered to people suffering from very severe depression. Only people who are suicidal or completely debilitated by depression are considered suitable for ECT therapy.

ECT treatment involves sending electrical impulses into the brain. These electrical impulses cause a seizure to occur. The patient is under an anesthetic while this happens and awakens with no memory of the event. Sometimes upon awakening they are confused and nauseous. However, the memory loss is temporary.

Normally ECT is administered 6-12 times with each treatment separated by a few weeks. Many patients notice improvement after a few sessions.

Only when it is absolutely necessary is ECT therapy given. If it is thought that the depression needs to be addressed immediately, ECT is a consideration.

Taking Bipolar Depression Seriously

An extremely common and unfortunately, in my opinion, the worst form of depression is Bipolar. A person with Bipolar will experience recurring mood swings and recurrent highs and lows. Their conduct will take on an unpredictable form and they can go from happy to sad within seconds. A person suffering with Bipolar can get irritable over the smallest slightest things, often something unimportant like the taste of the soup. Anger follows with an unpleasant presentation of words. This can be a symptom of Bipolar. Unfortunately, this can last for a week and is not confined to a single day.

When a depressed person experiences a low feeling, it could be compared with real depression. There are a multitude of negative feelings that occur in a person's mind; like being unable to enjoy life and other people, feeling hopeless and guilt ridden, feeling unloved and extreme negativism. It is generally considered that if this persists for longer than one a week, a person can be diagnosed as Bipolar.

TREATING BIPOLAR

Bipolar depression is most prevalent can very severe. However, the good news is that it can be treated. Don't worry about it, but ensure that the depressed person contacts a therapist who can advise him/her with appropriate treatment and medication. Regular visits with a therapist are important so the person can interrelate and talk about his/her feelings which he/she may not find possible with family and friends.

Beneficial relief is a possibility using natural treatments, but for any permanent relief it is strongly recommended that you consult with a cognitive behavior therapist experienced in dealing with Bipolar. They will be capable of diagnosing your condition and delve deeply into your past and current behaviors. They are better equipped to deal with your situation, and will prescribe any necessary medication they feel you need. Frequent visits to your therapist will instill confidence and enable you to cooperate fully. With their experience of dealing with cases such as yours, they will be able to provide you with the pros and cons treatments and advise you on what treatment they feel is best for you. You must keep in mind that each person is different, and what may be good for one may not be best for you. So, seek the best therapist in the field and get the treatment you need.

Of the many natural methods used to relieve depression one is the relaxation technique; this is recognized to treat the observable symptoms that are affecting you. Through relaxation you can normalize your heart rate and you will regain your focus allowing you to concentrate. Relaxation can also reduce your blood pressure and eradicate those dark thoughts that so often lead to depression.

This natural relaxation treatment can be done in the comfort of your home and it will help you reduce anxiety and get de-stressed. This will also give you an increased spurt of energy and help improve your sleep. Thus you be able to deal with your daily in a calmer and more controlled manner.

This method teaches you to relax your muscles and relieve tension in your whole body. This method has existed for over 50 years. When one I sin a depressed state of mind it affects relationships with people close to you. Relaxing your muscles helps to relieve tension and your mind clears and focuses allowing you to relate better with people around you.

Utilizing this method of relaxation, your muscles will tighten, so to achieve your goal requires practice. As your body loses its tension, your mind will improve and your ability to focus and concentrate will be improved and you will discover that you will be less stressed and anxious.

A crucial point of this natural method is that it must be practiced on a regular basis and not sporadically if it is to produce benefits. A daily commitment must be decided on and kept up. Along with this, you can include meditation, which is proven to clear your mind and fill it serene and peaceful thoughts.

Also another great method of relaxation is yoga. Yoga is also beneficial for your body and mind because it is soothing and removes stress from your system. The key is to practice regularly.

Just Don't Bother Me!

Levels of depression range from mild to severe accompanied by suicidal thoughts Mild depression can express itself in different ways like overeating or being anti-social, major depression on the other hand can put one's life on hold. Life will seem to have no purpose or joy. In fact, many simply want to stay in bed and not leave their house.

Television commercials tend to show persons struggling with major depression as indolently gazing out of the window, and when spoken to, the person is completely blanked out seemingly in a dark world of his own.

The Symptoms Of Major Depression

Many things in life are destroyed by major depression. You lack self-confidence, and this lack leads to retreating from society in general. You develop anti-social traits, push your family away and destroy relationships. Violence too, can be a part of this depression. Your lack of appetite may affect your physical well-being.

Major depressive order is the name applied to Major Depression. When you notice daily symptoms like sleeplessness, feel worthless and lacking confidence, tiredness and non-decisiveness even in petty matters, and these symptoms continue unceasingly for 2 weeks, then you are most likely going through a major depression episode.

Depressed people also harbor negative thoughts about themselves. For instance, a person may be choosing not to be with anyone and is essentially disinterested in things he previously enjoyed. There is also an overall feeling of indifference and lethargy reflecting a negative state of mind.

The number one thing to always be on the alert for is a person thinking about suicide because a feeling of hopelessness has set in.

Do not despair, help is available and with the correct diagnoses and treatment a cure can be realized. Extreme cases of depression will require medication and possibly other forms of treatment. The person can be calmed down with anti-depressants and once that is accomplished, he/she can progress to other treatments. The critical issue is to seek a competent therapist who can make the correct diagnosis and evaluate the person's requirements and put him/her on the road to recovery.

Are you Getting Anxious Over Anxiety Depression?

Many people try to take on too many tasks putting extra strain on them. This naturally leads to stress. Not only does it put a strain on the body, it affects the mind as well. In severe cases this can lead to a nervous break-down. There are also hyper active people who feel the urge to get things done on time. This too takes a toll on their physical and mental health.

People who are stressed out because they took on too many activities which they cannot deal with will tend to display nervousness and erratic behavior. They will experience mood swings as the pressure increases. People like this need to relax and face things in a tranquil manner if they wish to retain their sanity.

To make the most of visits with a therapist, you need to do some self-analysis of your thoughts and behavior. Doing so will be of benefit when you consult with a therapist and help in finding the right cure.

Various Types Of Depression

Depression comes in more than one flavor. **Bipolar** and **Cyclothemia** are similar because they both present as mood swings and they both present as frequent highs and lows. **Dysthimia** is less severe but needs to be treated quickly. There is **postpartum** depression which is caused by a huge amount of stress during childbirth coupled with the fear of child rearing. Postpartum also needs to be dealt with quickly.

As mentioned earlier, the most common depression is **Anxiety Depression**. While it is typical to worry about everyday occurrences, if a person is constantly worrying over anything and everything they need to visit a therapist.

Generalized Anxiety Disorder is indicated when a person exhibits an inordinate and unreasonable sense of paranoia and is stressed out for no obvious reason. Other symptoms are inability to concentrate and focus, sleeplessness and inactivity. However, the good news is that treatment is available. If you have these symptoms you should visit a therapist. The therapist will in turn, diagnose your symptoms recommend appropriate treatment. It may require medication to help to calm your nerves but with a good therapist and the right medication you will soon be recovering.

TREATMENT BY MEDICATION

Medication is often prescribed for severe depression, but in many cases patients do not respond to so medication is not always applicable, but it depends on each individual case. Doctors only prescribe medication as a last resort. They prescribe medication only when a person is extremely depressed and is considering suicide or if a person is delusional and there is a possibility they could become violent. Medication may be prescribed for depression when nothing else has worked, they do not respond to psychotherapy or is uncontrollably violent.

TYPES OF MEDICATION

Various types of medication may be prescribed. The usual suspects are tranquilizers such as benzodiazepine, serotonin or tricyclics. These medications are prescribed of imbalances or shortages of chemicals in the brain that result in dysfunctional neurotransmitters, which results in excess worry and stress.

There are a great number of tranquilizers and anti-depressants on the market that are used to treat depressed people. Many of these medications have negative, unpleasant side effects so they should not be continued. Additionally, some medications are addictive and must be withdrawn slowly.

Certain medications are available that do not produce the same outcome as anti-depressants. This is because they do not address the same chemicals yet they do have a positive effect on moods and they can stabilize them.

Medication is not advisable for everyone. This is especially true if a person is pregnant or if a person is taking some other medication and the two cannot be mixed. Whenever possible, it is preferable to treat the root cause of the problem with considered counseling. Only if there is no change and or the condition worsens should medication be prescribed. Medications for depression are very potent and often come with some nasty side effects. As a result, a lot of people quit. Then, when the condition relapses, there is no option other than to start taking the medication again.

DIFFERENT FORMS OF DEPRESSION

Some forms of depression go back a long way and the causes may be traced all the way back to one's childhood. If when you evaluate your anxiety, stress and worry you feel they happen all too often, then it may be time to seek professional help. By identifying and pinpointing your emotions you will gain an understanding and can decide whether or not you should visit a doctor.

DEPRESSION TEST BASICS

Depression tests, allow you to identify your symptoms. Since a lot of depressed people are unaware that their feelings and thoughts border on the morbid they are in a state of depression. Their life is gradually changing and the reasons may be due to various factors.

Anybody experiencing depression can take a depression test. The test determines whether or not your symptoms have lasted for more than 2 weeks. If they have, it is a pretty reliable sign that you need to see a doctor who can help you.

The Symptoms To Look For Are:

Melancholic thoughts that just pop up, feelings of worthlessness and thinking that nobody would miss you if you were gone, difficulty making decisions, putting things off, shamefulness, the inability to enjoy oneself with friends, lethargy, not enjoying being with your family, you don't want to eat, over or under sleeping and apathy.

Depression affects both mental and physical health as well as relations with relatives and close friends. After taking a depression test, the next step is to begin monitoring your moods, and make notes of any changes in your behavioral patterns.

Causes Of Depression

Countless studies have been done on depression, and many theories have been offered up explain why people descend into a state of depression. The general consensus is that there are a variety of causes of depression and no single factor.

A lot of doctors believe depression could be genetic. These doctors believe certain qualities will reappear in following generations. It appears that the only deduction depression researches can conclude is that many factors contribute to depression, and that by removing these factors one by one, treatment can be successful.

CHILDHOOD EXPERIENCES

Doctors delve totally into a person's childhood to try to discover factors that may constrain a person. As an example, if a person has experienced discomfort in either physical or sexual areas, this will in all likelihood have a direct influence on a person's emotional health. The future will often seem uninviting and a feeling of self-unimportance can prevail. The person often will be withdrawn on a social basis and have a habit of isolating himself.

Depression may also be an organic factor. We must keep in mind that chemicals are present in the brain that helps us to safeguard against endangerment. Our reflexes enable us to defend ourselves, but if there is an imbalance of chemicals, then we are unable to react as rapidly. Additionally, keeping emotions quiescent ultimately brings out melancholic thoughts and feelings and a powerlessness to handle any forms of anxiety or stress.

MEDICAL CONDITIONS AND DRUGS AS A CAUSE OF DEPRESSION

There are certain conditions such as hyperthyroidism that may seriously affect the capability of a person to handle situations such as job loss or the loss of loved ones. Panic attacks occur frequently because the person is incapable of handling any emotional knock-back. Effectively handling pain can be problematic under these conditions.

Cocaine and drugs like it may have an overwhelming effect on the brain. They can impair brain cells, cause paranoia and yield imbalance thus putting a person in a constant state of apprehension and fright. Humans are complex, so as to effectively treat depression it is vital that the beginnings of the problem are explored. Depression may have its origins in one's childhood experiences, job loss or the loss of a loved one. All these potential causes need to be addressed and dealt with. Bolstered by medication and other available treatments, you should be able to return to a normal life.

Symptoms Of Clinical Depression

Diagnosing clinical depression is difficult because sufferers do not behave in an abnormal manner. They do not maintain long silences or fail to get ready for their day. In truth, most people who are clinically depressed are not aware that they are depressed. Thus it is very difficult for doctors to identify that the individual is suffering from depression.

A doctor's primary focus and what they rely on most is finding the cause. The brain is important because it transmits information and messages through neurotransmitters which are controlled by chemicals like Dopamine and Serotonin. When these chemicals are not produced in certain quantities the neurotransmitters cannot work. This results in a chain reaction affecting the person's thought processes until depression sets in. To successfully treat a clinically depressed person one must first analyze past and present behavioral patterns. For instance, it could be that they do not want to socialize which was something they enjoyed in the past.

There may also be symptoms like an elevation in blood pressure or weight changes.

Other symptoms may be affecting their mind generating feelings of futility. Negative thoughts pervade their mind and these show themselves in a person's demeanor. Oft times they feel life is not worth living. Everything appears valueless, there is no joy, and there is nothing to look forward to. They focus on the mistakes they have made and seem to be unable to lead a normal life. If any of this describes you, then you are in all likelihood going through a period of depression.

Sometimes people will act in a manner that displays fear and worry by crying or being overly fearful. They may not care about participating in group functions or attending parties, and if they do, they tend to remain aloof. They might decline to be drawn into any topic and simply prefer their own company.

Sometimes clinical depression exhibits itself in mania and mania definitely requires immediate treatment. If mania is not treated, it will worsen the situation and soon become a cause for alarm. If your mind is full of negativity, and you are blaming yourself for all your blunders, you do not want to spend time with those close to you and your body has undergone a change then you should visit your doctor and ask to be referred you to a specialist who can evaluate your needs and help you accordingly.

CHRONIC DEPRESSION

Chronic depression can last for a long time and a person can experience this on and off. It never really goes away entirely but keeps recurring even though it may not be severe. Different methods of treatment are tried by therapists, such as group therapy and counseling prescribing medication. Some people respond to this treatment and avoid medication, but for some, the only option is medication which is not a permanent solution.

DYSTHYMIA

Dysthymia, another form of chronic depression is not a severe illness. Dysthymia does not keep you dysfunctional, but it does reveal itself in a variety of ways. Dysthymia exhibits itself by a lack of concentration, feelings of hopelessness, thoughts of suicide and a total lack of confidence. These feelings are constant and can last for long periods or even years.

Dysthymia can begin at any time in a person's life. Dysthymia is not limited to any single age group; it can affect the young and the old alike. Dysthymia displays no visible symptoms that have an effect on bodily functions and a person is able to do his work so it is extremely difficult to diagnose. However, Dysthymia cannot be neglected, as it will not just fade away, so treatment should be sought.

If the treatment is begun early, it will halt Dysthymia and prevent it from growing to something that will need to be treated with medication. Many cases of Dysthymia do not respond to treatment, but do not give up. There are various other forms of treatments or therapies that a psychiatrist will be able to recommend.

It is most important that you to recognize that you are feeling down and are not enjoying life or you are having a tendency to avoid people because you are lacking confidence. You should also consider the length of time that you have felt this way and the indications that seem to be appearing that are preventing you from living a full life. Once these conditions have been identified you can progress the next level which is seeking help.

The Truth About Postpartum Depression

Postpartum Depression is a severe illness that requires study so as you can be knowledgeable of its dangers. Pregnancy is a trying time and the thought of raising a baby along with the responsibilities involved in rearing a child is something that for some people who are not strong willed can be frightening. Even though a person may avoid alcohol and smoking, excessive exercise and stress, negative thoughts can affect the baby.

Reasons For Postpartum Depression

Although the causes of postpartum depression have been discovered and steps have been taken to eliminate it through either medication or counseling it can still be prevented. New mothers are particularly vulnerable and postpartum depression is very similar to depression.

Childbirth can be both physically and mentally stressful. The body experiences hormonal changes which can be uncomfortable while simultaneously affecting a person's moods. This is the primary cause of postpartum depression. New mothers who have been reluctant to have children and see it as fearful, are the most likely to suffer postpartum depression. Rather than being happy at the thought of having a baby and motherhood, they envision it as something that will manifest strain, pain and stress.

If a person is suffering with postpartum depression, it is crucial that they see a therapist, as the child can be hurt by the mother's angry feelings towards them. She will blame the child for all her problems like being overweight and unappealing. It is utterly critical to seek the counsel of a good therapist who will, if all else fails, put her on medication. Postpartum depression can be the cause of murder. Typically the mother is ignorant of what is happening in her head and sees the child as responsible for all her troubles. In order to avert a tragedy, it is best to seek out a good therapist to guide and help you to move forward.

AVOIDING THE SIDE EFFECTS OF MEDICATION

Conquering depression is very difficult. Depression leaves some people absolutely useless and without hope of a future. Others become housebound and yet others take their own lives. The effects of depression manifest in different ways in different people. Some sufferers are fine for a period of time and then slide into a state of depression. Some depressed people suffer a more chronic condition.

Depression is treatable but it may require more than one kind of therapy. Whichever therapy it is, it will take time to become effective. Some people do not want drug treatments. While drug treatments can be quite effective they can afflict you with numerous side effects. Depression can be treated in a natural manner and a natural way is normally the first course of action.

One essential is getting good night's sleep. There is a close link between sleep and mood. Tiredness causes people to react to things in a different way than we do when we have had enough sleep.

You should avoid caffeine and other stimulants. Though they may give you short bursts of energy, they have been known to diminish serotonin levels.

If your lifestyle causes you to skip meals take a daily multivitamin

Getting in touch with your spiritual side can be beneficial so you may want to try that. Getting in touch with your spiritual side can be done in a variety of ways. Going to church is a good opportunity if you enjoy that. You may want to consider meditation also well. One does not need to be religious to be spiritual.

Another good thing is more exercise. This doesn't mean training for a decathlon. Start slowly and work your way up as you feel comfortable. Exercise releases endorphins which give you a feeling of greater empowerment.

Treating depression can be challenging. Many sufferers are disinclined to take medications because of the side effects. The natural approach is less demanding on your body and will provide other health benefits.

If you are inclined to do so, try treating depression the natural way first. The other methods will still be there if it fails.

RECOGNIZING DEPRESSION

There are many factors which cause depression. Two primary factors are stress and fatigue. Our body's react differently when we are stressed than they do when we are relaxed. Depression is only one of many illnesses it can lead to. When a body is under excessive stress for too long it will ultimately shut down and the person ceases to operate in the same capacity.

Completely avoiding stress in our lives is impossible. Everybody is experiencing stress some of the time. Stress can be healthy at times, however, continuous stress will eventually produce negative effects which can in due course, result in chronic depression.

Chronic fatigue is common with people who are under constant stress, they seem to always be tired and run down. Stress depletes energy sources and leaves the body feeling drained of energy. This dangerous symptom is directly linked to depression.

Sometimes depressed people express anger at people making demands. Everybody over reacts at some time or another but if the anger is excessive over the slightest request this person needs a break.

Sometimes people are overly self-critical. They may be angered at themselves for letting things heap up or for ceding to everyone else's demands. Being angry with oneself has been linked to depression so this is a sign that should set the alarm bells ringing.

Sometimes people display feelings of extreme paranoia when they are faced with incredible stress and they feel like they are being beleaguered. At times like this, they believe the world is out to get them.

Irrational thought are also a sign of depression. Keep a close watch on anyone displaying this behavior.

Frequent headaches or gastrointestinal problems are also a sign they are under too much stress and can lead to serious health problems if they don't slow the pace.

Stress is one of the leading causes of depression and recognizing the warning signs can make the difference between treating severe depression or simply coping with stress. If you are showing these symptoms or you know someone who is, encourage them to seek help.

Helping Someone Else More

When a person struggling with depression lives with you, you obviously want to help them all you can. You'll naturally feel a need to offer all of the support possible and try to assist their recovery. Left untreated, depression can and does destroy families and lives. Nevertheless, it is important that you set aside take for yourself as well.

You must be prepared for personality changes and changes of behavior. The depressed person may not want to participate in things they previously enjoyed. The depressed person may reject you emotionally and/or sexually. This does not equate to them not loving you anymore. It is merely the depression. Exercise patience and show that you are supportive. It is a difficult time but with time, patience and treatment it should pass.

Often a depressed person will withdraw to a point where the simplest of tasks become too difficult to deal with. Basic tasks like bill paying, shopping and housework become just too much for them to cope with. You may need to do these tasks yourself for a while but you must at all times, keep in mind that this is a malady and all the support you provide give will assist in their recovery.

If a person who is depressed is ever going to get well treatment is essential. They may be reluctant to go, they may forget to attend sessions or to take medications. They will probably need reminders and encouragement to go. If the forgo treatment they certainly will not improve and will probably get worse.

Depression tends to remove hope. Depressed people often feel that their life is never going to be different and that nothing will be better in the future. They need constant reminders that there is hope and proffer it any way possible.

Anger is an emotion you will experience and it is appropriate to tell them that you are angry with their illness not them. It is vitally to separate the two. If they believe you are angry with them it will probably worsen their symptoms.

Finally, keep things in perspective. You cannot cure the depression so don't kid yourself into believing you can. Though depression will influence your life, don't let it take it over.

Depression In The Workplace

Depression can affect anyone and knowing the signs is the first step in treating them. Many cases of depression are a result of the workplace. Those in highly stressful or undesirable jobs can be susceptible to workplace depression.

Getting an education about depression is step one. If any employee is suffering from depression, though their condition is controlled, they will in all likelihood not be your best employee. Be alert for low productivity but always remember that this isn't a personality flaw, it is an illness.

Sometimes depressed people cease caring about their personal safety. If you notice someone taking unnecessary risks then consider it as a sign. Additionally, if they appear to be highly accident prone consider this as another indicator.

Anticipate frequent mood changes, the person may go from anger to sadness and then become uncooperative.

You should anticipate low morale. If the person seems complain about several facets of their life then depression is a strong possibility.

If the person appears to be frequently tired, this could be a cause for concern. Chronic fatigue is common with depression. If the person appears to be tired all the time or is always complaining of fatigue then you should be concerned.

If an employee has many absences, this too may be a sign of depression. Depressed people will use with colds and flu symptoms as an excuse because no one will accept depression as a valid reason.

Sometimes depressed people will self-medicate using drugs and alcohol. This is a problem needs to be dealt with immediately.

Workplace depression is a real phenomenon that can be treated. As an employer, step one is recognition of the signs. Next, educate yourself about depression. Finally, encourage your employee to seek professional help. These are some of the most effective things an employer can do to combat workplace depression.

Depression is a very destructive illness. It puts stress and strain on both families and relationships, in addition to loss of productivity it can cause in the workplace. Depression causes employers to lose money.

No employer can treat or cure depression but there are things that can be done to help.

Be aware of decreased productivity. If a person was previously a good worker and you notice a decline in their productivity this can be especially worrying. There could be a basic cause and depression is a very real possibility.

People who are depressed quite often ignore warnings of stress. This can result in the symptoms manifesting in a physical way. If employee is regularly complaining of aches and pains then depression could be the cause.

Speaking with the employee, they need to know that they are expected to be productive. Tell them you have noticed the changes and are concerned but do not make them feel that their job is in jeopardy. Believing their job is in jeopardy will probably make things worse. If you have access to employee assistance programs, encourage the person to use them.

Additionally, you need to set clear guidelines about what your expectations of the person. Tell them about the company's policy regarding depression related illnesses and what support they can expect.

Assure the employee that everything is confidential and that even you are not entitled to know what happens in counseling sessions. If the employee decides to get help you may have to accommodate a more flexible work schedule. This time will be returned eventually through increased productivity.

Severe depression can result in very serious consequences. Any talk of suicide should be taken seriously, report it immediately and they will thank you for it later.

LIGHT THERAPIES

Depression destroys lives. The lives of people suffering from depression are of course affected but the lives of the people close to him or her are affected also. The strain is felt almost as much by families and loved ones as the sufferer. Work and social contacts can suffer as well.

Luckily, we know lot more about depression today. The approach is to treat it as an illness not as a disorder. There are many treatments for depression and sometimes several or a combination of treatments may be needed before any improvement is realized.

Light is known to reduce the levels of melatonin in the brain. Melatonin is a chemical that can cause the blues and depression. A lot of improvement has been seen in many depression patients by spending at least 4 hours a day sitting in front of a bright light. One can conduct light therapy using a light box. Many people get depressed with the changing of the seasons as the days get shorter and the weather gets gloomier. This reduces the amount of exposure to natural sunlight so our serotonin levels begin dropping. This change affects everyone's mood but for a person suffering from depression it will seem a great deal worse. The person is required to sit in front of the light box. They can do whatever they wish to do provided they stay within 2-3 feet of the light box. The light helps replace the serotonin levels and reduces the chances of serious depression.

Depression is an illness that destroys individuals as well as families. When a person becomes seriously depressed they often cease to function in a normal manner. Everyone who is close to a person who is depressed will be affected. Fortunately there are many different therapies that can be tried.

Anxiety Depression

Some people's personalities are more prone to causing anxiousness than others.

The main cause is constant stress, constant stress causes anxiety and an overdose of anxiety often leads to anxiety depression. People who are expressing anxiety regularly display some common traits.

They include the following:

Constantly striving for perfection.

Feeling like a failure when they don't achieve their goals.

Nervousness.

They often feel guilty about what they did or did not do.

They don't like to hear any criticism about themselves.

They display obsessive traits.

They often invent things to worry about.

If your thinking is constantly leading you to self-criticism, you can develop anxiety depression. If you recognize that you have an anxiety susceptible personality, you can avoid slipping into depression and even if you already suffer from anxiety depression, you can learn to change your thinking.

Often anxiety depression is self-induced. The reason, you're so hard on yourself that you can never be a winner in your thoughts. You strive to be perfect yet no one is perfect. You try to be all things to all, and that is impossible. It is because of these feelings and thoughts that you are never satisfied and you begin to tell yourself that you're a worthless failure.

There are varying levels of anxiety depression that people experience. Some have a mild case that affects their attitude toward themselves, but does not interfere with their activities. Some have a severe form of anxiety depression driving them deeper and deeper into a pit of discontent. The key in any treatment is to change your self-perspective and cognitive and behavioral therapies can help.

One of the more common indications of anxiety depression is harboring a belief that you can't explain it because you think that people won't like you. That very lack of self-esteem makes you always place yourself after everybody else. You also probably have anticipations that are way too high putting any success way beyond your reach.

During therapy you will learn to set realistic goals and to accept the end results of your effort in a positive way.
Anxiety depression can be debilitating if left unchecked. You have to learn to like yourself first.

Every person, including you has special talents and abilities. If you focus your energy onto exploiting those abilities rather than quashing them, you will be astounded at how quickly you can rise above your depression. Thoughts can be either helpful or self-defeating so choose your thoughts wisely.

CHILDHOOD DEPRESSION

It would seem that childhood depression should not exist, because childhood should be filled with thoughts of family, friends and school, not worry and anxiety. Yet, sadly it is an increasing problem for many reasons. First, because they are human, children are subject to the same problems as adults. Children, due to genetics, may be born with a predisposition towards depression, have family problems and suffer stress.

Childhood depression shows itself in various ways. Any child can experience repeated high and low emotional states. Depressed children often don't want to go outside to play with friends. If a child's school performance changes, when he or she was doing well in school and has lost interest, it can be a sign of depression. Another oft seen symptom is lack of interest in ordinary activities.

Childhood depression is treatable. If any parent thinks their child might be depressed they can take certain steps to re-involve the child in a number of ways. First you should try to get your child interested in some activity; it can be a hobby, social or athletic activity or certain toys.

Another very important step is to have regular conversations with the child. During these conversations, be wary of reacting in a critical manner. Childhood depression usually means the child is suffering with low self-esteem. Your mission should be to build upon feelings of self-worth which will strengthen coping mechanisms.

It's a good idea to try working with your child to develop appropriate responses to different situations. Life is always going to present moments when one must overcome a perceived failure or difficult situation. If you child has not been taught how to respond and constantly gets frustrated, then childhood depression can set in.

If your child is suffering with depression, you need to try to uncover the causes. If he or she is experiencing difficulty at school there may be a problem between your child and another child. If your child unexpectedly withdraws with no apparent cause, then it might be appropriate to have your child visit a therapist to investigate the issues. A common cause of depression in children is an unknown learning disability.

Most young children are not capable of communicating their thoughts and feelings so you have to make an extra effort to "understand" the situation. There are many treatment options if the self-help treatments don't work.

Clinical Depression

If you are diagnosed as clinically depressed, a variety of treatment options are available. They include behavior and cognitive therapy, medication and interpersonal therapy. Parts of the therapy can be undertaken by you without the assistance of a doctor. You can learn to stop negative thoughts about your talents, abilities and self-esteem. You can maintain a diary or force yourself to become more active. But for most people, clinical depression requires treatment by a specialist.

When treat clinical depression doctors often combine medication with one or more other therapies. The goal being to keep medication levels as low as possible with the goal of eventual cessation.

During controlled studies, cognitive therapy has proven to be quite effective in treating depression. Cognitive therapy, teaches you to start loving yourself by changing your opinions.

Interpersonal therapy includes counseling that is focused on other people or events involving other people that may have initiated your depression. Interpersonal therapy can also work to boost your self-esteem allowing you to have better interpersonal relationships.

Behavior therapy will help you to alter your self-defeating behavior and you learn to enjoy being involved with activities again. Behavior therapy is often used in conjunction with cognitive therapy.

Several medications are commonly used to treat clinical depression. Among them are Selective Serotonin Reuptake Inhibitors (SSRI) and Tricyclics. Whenever someone has suicidal thoughts, anti-depressant medications are almost always prescribed. In other situations, medications may be prescribed short-term to provide a head start on cognitive and behavior therapy.

Of course, only a medical doctor can prescribe drugs for clinical depression. But there are psychotherapists who offer other treatment options. The people are clinical psychologists and psychiatrists. Psychiatrists, as medical doctors, are able to prescribe medication and also provide group, behavior and cognitive.

What is Clinical Depression

Depression is a mental illness that is often characterized by extended periods of melancholy and sadness according to experts from the field of psychiatry.

However, if a person is moping around and generally hating the world it does not mean they have depression, but if the behavior and feelings of emptiness, hopelessness and loss of self-worth goes on and on that individual is indeed depressed.

There are many types of depression:

Bipolar, is characterized by sudden and extreme mood changes where one minute he/she is in a state of euphoria then the next minute/day/week he/she is feeling as though they are in a personal hell.

Postpartum depression, experienced by new mothers is characterized by prolonged periods of sadness and feelings of emptiness due to physical and mental stress during pregnancy and child birth, an ambiguous sense of concern towards the new born baby can be just some of the possible reasons new mother go through this.

Dysthimia has a slight similarity to depression, although it's been proven to be a lot less severe, but of course should be treated immediately.

Cyclothemia has a slight similarity to Bipolar wherein the individual struggling from this mental illness may infrequently suffer from severe mood changes.

Seasonal Affective Disorder is characterized by finding oneself in a rut but only during specific seasons, studies however, prove that more people actually suffer more during the winter and autumn.

Mood swings, are displayed when a person's mood may change from happy to sad then to angry in a very short time.

Clinical depression however, or what some call 'major' depression, is the actual medical term for depression. Clinical depression is actually more of a disorder since it essentially covers only those who are suffering symptoms related to depression. Clinical depression is fundamentally just a medical term. However, though it is not an actual disorder, Clinical depression is still treated. Patients who have sought treatments for Clinical depression have proven to be quite successful in their pursuit because about 80 percent of Clinical depression patients have

been treated and have found relief from the
disorder.

HELPING YOURSELF WITH DEPRESSION

If you're currently totally out of your normal system and just basically ignoring or hating almost everything and anyone, make an effort to get yourself checked by a psychiatrist soon. Those little mood swings and erratic behaviors that you've been trying to ignore for a while may actually be symptoms of depression. Act fast because if you don't it will be a lot harder for you to be able to get yourself cured, especially once self-delusion starts raise its ugly head.

Start by hauling your depressed rear-end to the hospital and get yourself diagnosed by a qualified psychiatrist who will help you with your concerns, answer any questions that you may have and provide you with the best available depression treatment. All you need is courage and the right attitude.

In spite of how scary or daunting a task, when traveling the road towards sound mental health and recovery from depression help is plentiful. It is up to you if you're willing to take in some of that depression help, whether it be from your friends, family or a support group but it starts with yourself.

The old proverb, "slowly but surely" prominently applies in treating depression.

Do not assume that depression can be treated in a snap. Depression help starts by trying to understand the patient's situation and continuous patience as well as always extending your help. Depression help is never easy and neither is the treatment, which is why both the patient and his/her loved ones need to help each other every step of the way. Never set goals that are unachievable or unrealistic. Do not be too hard on yourself and believe that you are good and strong enough to achieve your goals one step at a time.

DEPRESSION MEDICATIONS

Because depression medications are strong drugs that influence your brain functioning they are serious business, some medications are even addictive so they're not to be taken lightly. There's a good reason that all antidepressant medications are strictly controlled and need to be taken only under the supervision of a doctor.

Not every person wants to resort to medications for relief. Each individual must talk with his/ her doctor to decide which course of treatment is right for them. Some individuals try many other forms of treatment initially, yet others begin with a combined treatment of medication and one or more other therapies.

So how do you determine when starting to take a depression medication is the best option? The first determination most doctors will make is how long you have been depressed and which, if any, therapies you have tried. Other considerations in the decision to use medication include religious values, other medications you are currently using, pregnancy and susceptibility for drug dependency. As you can see, it can be a difficult and complex decision.

We too frequently see drugs as a quick cure all for everything that ails us. Be aware that even if you and your doctor decide drugs are the best option, they don't deliver instant gratification. You may have to take the medications for many months and it can take a few weeks before you will notice any changes.

One of the primary things to consider before deciding to use medications is the severity of the disorder. If you are suffering with Bipolar or are depressed for at least 2 hours each day, you have severe depression. If depression is affecting your work and generating other problems in your daily life, medication might be prescribed right away. One good thing about medication is it can be stopped in the future. You can use it for the months that you need it and then as your depression decreases, you can begin to withdraw from the drugs.

Non-medication treatments require a change in thinking and lifestyle for the long term. Using medications should be, but is not always, a short term solution.

When you start using medication, you may need to experiment with more than one to find what works best for you. When taking medications you need constant doctor supervision because most the drugs have side effects, but these side effects are different for everyone.

DEPRESSION TEST

Sometimes it can be hard to tell the difference between the normal emotional ups and downs that people experience and depression. But when you start to think that you should feel better about yourself and your world than you do, taking a depression test can provide some insight.

Depression does not come in only one flavor. In terms of symptoms, it can take many different forms, and no two individuals are the same. But there are common symptoms that often occur and they can serve as gauges of your emotional health. Taking a depression test can help you decide whether or not you need to talk to a doctor.

A depression test is merely a checklist of symptoms you or someone else identifies as being applicable to you. It is surprising how many people don't know that they have a mild case of depression and some don't even realize how much their life has changed.

The depression test can be used by an individual who suspects they might be suffering with depression or even by family or friends who don't know how to identify depression in someone they love. The general guideline is to consider if you have experienced any of the following list of symptoms for longer than 2 weeks.

He/she thinks their life is out of control
He/she believes their life is not important
He/she is convinced no one would miss them if they were to die
He/she can't make even small decisions
He/she doesn't expect anything at all to be enjoyable
He/she constantly feels ashamed
He/she experiences frequent and unexplained crying
He/she doesn't enjoy being with friends or attending events
He/she has stopped exercising
He/she has given up things once enjoyed
He/she avoids people whenever possible
He/she feels alone all the time
He/she doesn't enjoy being with family anymore
He/she feels like no one understands them
He/she has losing their appetite
He/she is unable to sleep or sleeping too much
He/she has no energy

A depression test can actually include a lot more symptoms, but this provides a good idea of the kinds of things you should consider.

As you can see in the list, depression touches more than only your emotions.

Once you have taken the depression test, the next thing to do is to begin tracking mood changes by creating a mood diary. A mood diary is something very tangible and quite convincing to show your doctor or therapist.

Finding The Right Depression Medication

Are you always feeling down? Are you always in the mood to be alone rather than be with others and have a good time? If you have been suffering from prolonged sadness you must face these bouts of depression visit a psychiatrist. Psychiatrists are doctors who really can help you with your problem.

Depression can be cured, especially if it is diagnosed early, people with depression can be treated with therapy and medication. Although it may be expensive, sound mental health is worth every cent. Cognitive behavioral and interpersonal talk are healthy depression treatments and they are just two of the available depression treatments. Both actually produce fruitful and positive results even from short-term sessions.

Before starting on depression medication the patient must first get himself/ herself to a reliable doctor and get diagnosed for which type of depression the patient is actually suffering from. It may be clinical depression, Bipolar or one of the others. It's best to be sure of what you're actually dealing with because various medications are available in the market.

It is important to get the most appropriate one that'll actually cure your illness.

There's a wide variety of medications available to help treat people with depressive disorders. The most popular medications ones are the Selective Serotonin Reuptake Inhibitors (SSRIs). Also, there are Tricyclics and the other popular variant is Monoamine Oxidase Inhibitors (MAOIs). These medications are safer than Tricyclics because they have fewer side-effects.

Doctors frequently find it works better to mix up these medications depending on the needs of the patient. Additionally, the doses of medication can be increased or decreased depending on what is the most effective. Patients should never mix up medications or choose what dosage to take without first consulting their doctor.

Sedatives are not depression medication. Even though they are often prescribed as an adjunct to depression medication they will not cure one's illness. Their only purpose is to calm one's nerves.

There are common side-effects from depression medications. Usually they come from the Tricyclics. The most common side-effects are the following:

Dry mouth: It's best to always have some water nearby at all times so you have something to drink whenever dry mouth occurs.

Constipation: Eating and drinking high fiber will help to aid your digestion.

Blurry vision: This one's quite easy to pass but if it proves to be a lot of trouble consult your doctor immediately.

Headaches: Are a common problem with the most recent depression medication but they often pass quickly.

Insomnia: First-time users may experience this side-effect but it usually only lasts for a few weeks.

FINDING THE RIGHT DEPRESSION TREATMENT

Depression or persistent sadness is very common in the United States. About 9.5% percent of Americans suffer from this illness. Not all of them are treated so the effects of depression remain a burden to some people. Depression might seem simple to treat but it takes a lot more than a little cheering up to cure depression. Continual cognitive behavioral therapy is required in addition to taking all the medications the doctor prescribes. This doesn't come cheap, but the suffering that a person is going through due to depression is already reason enough for other people to start facing depression head on and pursue the various treatments that are available.

Often depression gets in the way of a person's day to day activities and his/her customary functions and the person's passion for life can quickly disintegrate. And, in place of a person's bright outlook is a person who dislikes his/herself, lacking self-confidence, trying to segregate themselves from other people and not caring much about living. Moreover, the individual struggling with depression isn't the only one who will be suffering. His/her loved ones will surely suffer too. By observing the person going through such hard times, not caring about anything or anyone, it's very probable that depression will not only destroy one's relationship with oneself but with his/her loved ones as well.

Treatment for depression starts with the person accepting his/her illness, just by being true to oneself, makes it a lot easier not only for the individual but for the doctor as well.

Psychotherapy is a popular type of treatment that includes short-term therapy sessions, normally requiring from ten to twenty weeks that promises to deliver positive results for the patient. This type of treatment helps the individual by slowly getting them to open up and discuss about their feelings and the source of their problems but more importantly the source of their illness. Healthy dialogues between a cognitive behavior therapist and the patient is a great treatment that will positively benefit the individual by encouraging him/her to talk about the stuff they've been keeping inside.

There are various medications available for treating depression that are great for helping the patient to normalize his/her mood swings, helping him/her sleep better and to be more pleasant towards others.

BIPOLAR DEPRESSION

Bipolar is also called manic-depressive illness.

Bipolar is a serious mood disorder and it is one of extremes. Bipolar is characterized by extreme highs and lows people with bipolar experience. Bipolar does not heal itself and must be treated. Abundant medical research studies have been and are being conducted about Bipolar, but currently treatments almost always include medication.

With depression, people will experience mostly low feelings. With Bipolar they go through extreme moods from the most ecstatic to deepest depression. During the ecstatic stage the individual is very happy and highly-strung. Their attention span is very short, sleeping is difficult and concentration is a chore. One of the most disturbing indicators during this ecstatic stage is a loss of good judgment and the tendency to be irresponsible. During the ecstatic stage a person may charge up all the credit cards, lose money gambling or involve themselves in risky business or sexual decisions.

In the depression stage, an individual with Bipolar will go through feelings of sadness and guilt. Their life becomes hopeless, suicidal thoughts can be manifested, he/she will have little interest in any activities and they may sleep a lot or very little.

Of course, no two people are the same. The ecstatic and depression highs and lows can in some cases be fairly mild, but the conduct during these times can devastate a family. A Bipolar depressive can and often does cause great financial and social problems among family members. People with Bipolar can also change moods in short periods of time. It's even possible to experience both ecstasy and depression at the same time.

Episodes of Bipolar can be triggered by various things. These include drug abuse and disturbing experiences such as the death of a loved one. There are varying treatments for Bipolar. The most common is prescription drugs that stabilize mood swings or act as antidepressants. Counseling sessions with a therapist is another common treatment. Therapists can assist people suffering with Bipolar by identifying when ecstatic or depression episodes are likely to happen. The objective is to decide if certain things cause the episodes to occur. Of course, there are other treatment methods but those are the two most common.

It's critical that you realize that Bipolar is a serious disorder requiring medical attention. Even though the research done seems to point to faulty neurotransmitters as the cause, it's not known for certain.

Natural Cure For Depression

Some people refuse to take prescriptions drugs unless it's a choice between living and dying. Instead, they would rather try a natural cure for their illness. There are a lot of natural products that people have used in an attempt to deal with depression. Whether or not they work, has yet to be scientifically proven in some cases, while others are known to be helpful.

Natural treatments for depression are considered to be any treatment that doesn't require prescription drugs. As an alternative, you may decide to try an herb or a supplement or simply make some changes in your diet. Additional natural treatments involve learning some relaxation techniques or having stress relieving massages. Regardless of what natural treatment you decide to use, it is still very important to inform your doctor. Depression is a serious illness and must never be taken lightly. A doctor will assist you in monitoring your headway while using natural alternatives.

There are choices for natural treatments and most people use more than one. A commonly used treatment is herbs and supplements. St.

John's wort is thought to work as a natural treatment for mild depression. St. John's wort is a perennial that's been used for hundreds of years in alternative treatments. Be aware at all times that herbs can interact with prescription medicines. That's another good reason why you should always inform your doctor of what you are taking.

Another natural cure that some people try is vitamins and minerals. One symptom of depression is a radical weight change. If you are not getting good nutrition the problem worsens. Depression affects the ability to concentrate and some vitamins and minerals such as vitamin B and Folic acid are said to be beneficial.

Changing your dietary habits is another natural treatment for depression. For example, Turkey has an amino acid which aids in the production of serotonin. Other beneficial foods are milk and potatoes. Foods high in omega-3 fatty acids such as soybeans and fish can be good for you. All of these foods assist with the chemical production of the brain. Ensure that you are getting good nourishment and hopefully you will decrease your depression.

There are many natural treatments for depression that individuals have tired. One of which is nerve stimulation. However one of the most popular treatments is to learn relaxation practices which may also include massages. One of the major causes of depression is excess stress and relaxation methods teach you how to manage and rein in anxious thoughts and reverse them. People who are both anxious and depressed often worsen their situation simply because they don't know how to relax. Having said that, there's no proof that it's true, but it certainly cannot hurt.

If you don't want to use medication and/or don't have enough time or money for traditional treatments, you should investigate trying natural treatments.

Postpartum Depression

Postpartum depression has been a disorder society has had a hard time accepting. After all, when you have a baby it should only bring great happiness to your life. Yet, being pregnant and having a baby is also a time when the body goes through enormous stress and hormones are produced in excess amounts. In most women this may cause some minor and unpredictable mood changes, but in others it's quite possible it creates postpartum depression.

Though hormones are the suspect, there's no definitive proof yet that hormones are the only culprit. Postpartum depression is a very serious disorder that affects women within weeks of giving birth. For some women, the depression begins after only a few days.

Postpartum depression becomes apparent when the new mother has difficulty accepting responsibility for the new infant. There may be lack of interest in the baby or quick irritation when the baby cries. Other symptoms of postpartum depression include the following.

Unable to sleep
Feelings of inadequacies
Exhaustion

Inability to cope with baby care
Despondency

The interesting fact is that a woman can complete an entire pregnancy with no signs of anxiety and then develop postpartum depression after birth. Some cases of postpartum depression are severe and include unexplained and frequent crying and even thoughts of suicide. The new mother has trouble functioning and can't seem to complete the smallest chores. Also, some women show lack of interest in the infant.

It's an unpleasant subject, but postpartum depression has been determined to be the cause of a mother injuring the infant or infant siblings. In the severest cases, postpartum depression can develop into a psychosis. A psychosis means the woman is probably hallucinating or has lost a grip on reality. In many of these cases brought to court, the new mother claims she heard voices telling her the baby or her other children must be killed.

The only reason this is discussed is because it's important to understand that postpartum depression is very real and must be treated. Ignoring the disorder does not make it go away. Fortunately, there are treatments that work well. In most cases, medication is prescribed by the doctor.

If you suspect you, or someone you know has postpartum depression, you should see a doctor immediately. Most women will experience some mild depression after the birth of a baby due to shifting hormones or the realization this child is now a continual responsibility. Before a baby is born, women get lots of concerned attention from family and friends. Once the baby comes, and the mother is doing fine, the attention stops and the work begins. But postpartum depression is a serious disorder that must be dealt with before symptoms worsen.

PSYCHOTIC DEPRESSION

All in all, psychotic depression is about the worst depression one can have. It's similar to major depression in that you lose touch with reality. Tragedy can transpire unless other people know what's happening in your mind. If you have ever watched the news you have seen mothers on trial for killing their children saying "God said it must be done because they are controlled by an evil entity". In other equally extraordinary trials, the devil has spoken to people and ordered them to commit inconceivable acts of violence.

There are several common symptoms associated with Psychotic depression. These are some of them:

They are hearing voices.
They are Delusional.
They Hallucinate.
They are Paranoid.
They suffer with Delusions.

When a person has Psychotic depression their reality is different from other people. They may believe ET is speaking to them on their cell phone. Or they think the voices they are hearing are instructing them to harm themselves. Obviously, they should not attempt to treat Psychotic depression on their own. Almost certainly they will require some hospitalization and definitely medication. A new medicine called atypical anti-psychotic is being used in cases of severe depression. These new medicines have produced results in cases where SSRIs and Tricyclics have failed. For people with Psychotic depression this is good news, because they often help individuals with the severest forms of depression. However, the bad news is there are have many possible side effects. Anyone taking one of these drugs requires constant monitoring. Here are some of the side effects.

Facial tics
Weight gain
Movement problems
Hypertension
Blurred vision

This list is not a comprehensive but it does give you a good idea of what side effects people go through when using atypical anti-psychotics. Regrettably, when a person is hallucinating or is suicidal, medications are necessary regardless of the unpleasant side effects.

The treatment for Psychotic depression is both long-term and complicated. When an individual is psychotic, they cannot monitor their own treatment.

If you know anybody experiencing any of the above symptoms it's imperative they seek treatment. It's treatable most of the time even though it's a complicated disorder. A doctor will in all likelihood prescribe medication in addition to other therapies. Other therapies could be group therapy or cognitive therapy.

Signs of Depression

There are many different signs of depression therefore it sometimes continues until the signs begin to form a pattern. The sooner you identify depression in yourself or someone else, the sooner you/they can begin treatment. Whether it's mild, severe or somewhere in between the two extremes it must be treated.

Some of the basic and common signs of depression are:

No feelings of self-worth
Low self- esteem
Don't like to be around other people, sometimes including family
Don't anticipate doing anything
Poor concentration
Feeling hopeless
Constant sadness
Thought of self-harm or suicide
Cannot make even simple decisions

An individual can experience one or more of these symptoms. Feeling sad for a few days is natural. It's normal to have stressful days. It's normal to experience days when life seems a little harder than it should be. What is not natural is to feel you are worthless or that the people in your life wouldn't miss you if you were gone. It is abnormal to be sad for more than a couple of weeks while experiencing constant fatigue and a general lack of interest in everything.

In many cases, the signs of depression are very noticeable. A person suffering from depression may cry a lot for no obvious reason. In extreme cases, they may refuse to get out of bed. In mild cases, people may be unable to make even simple decisions or is constantly feeling guilty. People suffering with depression can have trouble functioning both at work and home.

Some indicators of depression might not be severe and are therefore harder to recognize. One can suffer depression triggered by events like a death in the family or the loss of a job. On the surface they may appear to function normally but the signs of depression are there. One might cry at unexpected times or begin a corkscrew into unhappiness that eventually makes them non-functional.

Bipolar however has very obvious symptoms. While in a state of ecstasy, weird behavior such as foolish and harmful decision making becomes apparent. Whereas in the depressed state, there are feelings of hopelessness and all the frenzied activity stops. These states can and do happen over and over again and can even happen within a day.

The key to identifying depression is to look for patterns or constant worsening of the suspect symptoms. If the symptoms continue for more than a couple of weeks, seek professional help for you, your friend or family member.

THE TELL-TALE SYMPTOMS OF DEPRESSION

Individuals suffering from depression or manic disorders will exhibit every kind of symptom of depression that doctors tell you affect depressed. Often it's easy to overlook the symptoms and be unable to help oneself or others.

There are many symptoms of depression that depressed people may exhibit but they don't have to suffer from all of them before you encourage them to get diagnosed and be treated. Additionally, since the symptoms of depression vary, the timing of attacks also varies.

Below are some very common of symptoms of depression:

Any prolonged period of sadness or not feeling in the mood, people who are always not up to it and would rather just mope around the house and feel sorry for themselves are the best example for this symptom.

Feeling hopeless and an untiring pessimist: Talking of feeling sorry for oneself is a very common symptom of depression. As for the perpetual pessimist, people showing this symptom are most often very negative. Again, the feeling of hopelessness comes to mind.

Guilt, lost self-worth and helplessness: Other symptoms that can readily be seen on people who would rather sulk all day long are these. When an individual feels guilty over something, they become a very sad person who feels like they don't deserve happiness. Accordingly, the lost self-worth, if the person feels he/she isn't worthy of happiness or enjoyment, that's clear tell-tale symptom. Another contributor is helplessness. When supposing that things won't go your way, it's clear that you have absolutely no hope in your body.

Isn't interested in pleasure; dropping the hobbies, interests and other things that they used to enjoy: this tell-tale symptom shows how depressed someone can be, if someone is too sad to take any pleasure even in the things that they love then that person is completely lacking something and might well have caught the depression virus.

Fatigue, perennially tired: since they've lost whatever interest in life they may have had previously they are lacking physical energy all the time, if one prefers to just mope around, doesn't even eat or not get enough sleep, the person may well be on their way to depression.

Trouble concentrating, bad memory and indecisiveness: an individual suffering from depression easily exhibits this tell-tale symptom. When one's lack of interest in world or just about anything can lead to the individual losing track of things and not being able to remember things that happened or things that other people said. Lack of interest makes a depressed person very inattentive.

Of course there are more symptoms of depression that will help you see if a person (or yourself) needs to see a doctor to get some help: lack of sleep, too much sleep or waking up in the early hours of the morning are other symptoms of depression if they happen on a daily basis. Appetite loss and over eating may show one's lack of interest in life. Be wary of rapid weight loss or weight gain. Talking about death or wanting to die is a clear sign of depression. Restlessness and irritability are physical symptoms that are usually the result of poor mental health as are headaches, digestive disorders and various body pains.

TEEN DEPRESSION

Oftentimes teenagers can be hard to understand because they have many quite normal ups and downs as they begin to become adults. However, as evidenced by the ever increasing teen suicides teen depression is a growing problem. It's not uncommon to hear the parents of teenagers tangled up in violent acts in the schools, say the teen has been depressed. But it's difficult distinguish between the normal emotional inconsistency due to changes effected by hormones and true depression.

As the parent of a teenager, it's essential to watch for variations in behavior that don't make sense and seem to become worse. Teenagers that have always liked the company of friends and then stop socializing may be depressed. If they have lost interest in activities that one of the major signs of depression. Teen depression exposes itself in other ways also.

They lose interest in sports activities when previously sports were important.

Grades suddenly dropping at school.

Changes in dietary habits like loss of appetite or gluttonous eating.

Making comments indicating low self-esteem.

Mood fluctuations that are sudden

There are medical studies seeking the physical reasons for teen depression. A correlation has been found between obesity and depression. That makes perfect sense when you think about the symptoms in children. AS an example, obese children can suffer feelings of low self-worth due to being teased or bullied. Depressed teenagers may eat a lot of comfort food seeking consolation for their feelings of loneliness. Teenagers can experience problems at school and not discuss them with their parents. As a parent you thought things were fine only to learn there's been an unending problem between students or the student and teacher.

Teenagers can be very delicate people. The teens are the formative years, and when problems in socializing occur, it can be very discouraging. Sudden mood swings can also be an indicator that there's another problem in the teen's life. If a teenager is being harmed physically or sexually, depression can be the response.

Identifying teen depression is complex but not impossible. If you suspect your child is suffering with depression, try to talk to the child first. If the child won't talk to you then professional help may be necessary. It's imperative that some kind of treatment be started, since the loss of self-esteem can be overwhelming. Of course, one of the best treatments is lots of love!

TREATMENTS FOR DEPRESSION

There are a large assortment of treatments for depression and most often two or more are used at a time. Here is a list of the most common treatments used today.

Cognitive therapy
Group therapy
Medication
Behavioral therapy
Interpersonal therapy

Most depression treatments expect the person to keep notes as the first step and possibly an activity log. A log is a significant tool for both you and your therapist that helps to identify the depression triggers. It is also a worthy way to get your life back to normal.

One benefit of using notes and logs in the treatments is that it forces one to commence an activity to recover one's life. This is very important if depression has hindered your ability to think or operate in general. If one keeps a log of their feelings and thoughts, it becomes much easier to identify any negative thinking that gets out of control. A journal will expose things like feelings of failure and anxiety. Armed with the source of the thoughts, a good therapist can help you seek the reason for one's lack of self-esteem.

During any of the treatments an activity log is useful log keeping track of what needs to be done in one's life to keep it from sliding away. Depressed people often decide they don't care about anyone or anything. This can result in calamitous penalties if one doesn't pay his/her bills or deposit money in his/her bank account. Some people with depression neglect not only themselves they neglect significant tasks such as picking up the kids from school. Some even decide eating is too much of an effort. That's the reason some depressed people have sudden and severe weight loss.

When people are depressed their mind centers on dark thoughts that are most often self- critical. If one tells oneself they are incapable of doing anything right, the next logical thought is: "why try?" That is how the illness works. With the exception of medication, depression treatments assist people to change their thought patterns to see themselves as both capable and positive.

For someone who's never had depression it's impossible to comprehend how deep the mental hole can get.

Zoloft Depression

Zoloft depression is the number one, most-prescribed medicine for depression. With the introduction of this treatment the problems concerning depression can easily be gone.

Zoloft depression is proven to be a safe and extremely effective treatment for depression and anxiety. Zoloft depression has been around for about 14 years. Patients have responded well to treatments from Zoloft depression and doctors favor it's availability in various strengths, because of this someone suffering from depression doesn't have to settle for an alternative just because the dosage isn't available. With Zoloft depression, it's hard to not find the right dosage for you.

Zoloft is a type of medication which is known to people as a Selective Serotonin Reuptake Inhibitor (SSRI). It has a reputation of being a good treatment for people aged eighteen or above that are being treated for any of the following:

Depression
Panic disorder
Obsessive-compulsive disorder or OCD
Post traumatic disorder or PTSD

Premenstrual dysphoric disorder or PMDD
Social anxiety disorder

Zoloft isn't for everyone, patients who are already taking pimozide or MAOIs are sternly discouraged from using Zoloft depression. Zoloft medication has various side effects such as:

Diarrhea, nausea
Sleepiness/insomnia
Dry mouth
Sexual side effects.

According to studies many of people don't care about the side effects and opted to continue on taking Zoloft Depression.

A couple of good points to reflect on though are that Zoloft is not addictive and it is not in any way associated with weight gain.

Zoloft Depression comes in varying dosages, 25mg, 50mg and 100mg, so consult your doctor before taking Zoloft. One of the main reasons Zoloft was created in various dosages is that since each individual is unique, one person's need for Zoloft will differ from another person and that is the primary reason we need a doctor to assess how much or how little of Zoloft medication one really needs.

Depending on an individual's body or ability to respond to treatments along with the person's willingness to actually help himself/herself recover, the effects of Zoloft depression will be noticed in as little as 2 weeks. If you continue following the prescriptions as well as presenting yourself for every therapy session, Zoloft Depression will certainly help you.

A PREVIEW OF:

THE POISON DIET

INFORM YOURSELF BEFORE IT'S TOO LATE.

A.L HARLOW

INTRODUCTION

This book was written to help bring attention to the dangers of processed foods. Many people are unaware of the harmful chemicals they consume every day.

The FDA is not looking out for us, and manufacturers are not required to label dangerous additives in the foods they produce, no matter how bad they are.

With the knowledge you will gain from this book you will know what you are consuming and will be able to make intelligent choices regarding what you put in your mouth.

You and your family will live longer and stay healthier by not eating processed foods. Chemicals, like Glyphosate from Monsanto can be found in food, (even before processing) can give you cancer and other diseases.

What Are Processed Foods?

Not only microwave and other ready meals are processed foods. The phrase processed food, is in reference to any food that has been changed from its natural form in any way.

You may be consuming much more processed food than you are aware of.

Processed foods aren't by default unhealthy, but any food that has been processed might contain added salt, artificial flavoring, chemical preservatives, sugar and fat.

The major benefit of preparing food from scratch is that you know exactly what is going into it. However, even home cooked food often includes processed ingredients.

What is considered processed food?

You can be sure that most food bought in a shop has been processed in some form.

Here are some common processed foods.

Breakfast cereals

Cheese

Canned vegetables

Bread

Savory snacks including crisps

Meat products like bacon

Microwave meals or ready meals

Drinks, like milk or soft drinks

The techniques used in Food processing include canning, freezing, baking, pasteurizing and drying products.

When fruit and veg are frozen most of the vitamins are preserved, while tinned produce, without added sugar and salt, are convenient to store, cook and good to eat year round producing less waste and at a lower cost than fresh foods."

So what makes some foods less healthy when they are processed?

Additives like fat, salt and sugar are often added to processed foods to make them taste better and to extend shelf life.

This often leads to people consuming more than the safe amounts for these additives. This is because people may not know how much has been added to the food they are eating. These foods are frequently higher in calories because of the large amounts of added sugar or fat.

Furthermore, regularly eating more than 90g a day of red and processed meat has been linked to a greater risk of bowel cancer. Other studies have also indicated that eating large amounts of processed meat may be linked to an elevated risk of heart disease.

What is processed meat?

The term, "processed meat", means meat that has been preserved by curing, salting, smoking, or adding preservatives. Processed meats include bacon, sausages, ham, pâtés and salami.

The Department of Health recommends that you not eat more than 70g of red and processed meat a day. This equals a little over two slices of roast lamb, beef or pork or two or three rashers of bacon, with each being about equal in size to a half a slice of bread.

It's vitally important to remember that "processed" applies to a very broad range of food stuffs, many of which are okay to be eaten as part of a balanced diet.

How can I include processed foods in a healthy diet?

By reading the nutrition labels you will be able to make informed choices between processed products thereby keeping a close watch on the amount of processed foods that are high in fat, salt and added sugars that you are actually consuming.

Putting canned tomatoes in your shopping basket is a great way to improve your 5 a day. They can be stored longer and are less expensive than fresh tomatoes but first check the label to make sure they don't contain added salt or sugar.

Most of the pre-packaged foods have a nutrition label.

This nutrition label will include information on fat saturates, energy, carbs, protein, sugars and salt. The nutrition label may also give you information on nutrients such as fiber. Nutrition information is always based on a 100 gram serving and occasionally per portion.

How do I determine if a processed food is high in saturated fat, sugar or salt?

There are guidelines to tell you. These are:
Total fat
High = more than 17.5 grams per 100 grams
Low = 3 grams per 100 grams
Saturated fat
High = more than 5 grams per 100 grams
Low = 3 grams or less per 100 grams

For more books by this author please visit:

www.Al-Harlow.com

Printed in Great Britain
by Amazon

26418243R00066